To: _____

From: _____

Published by Sellers Publishing, Inc.
Text and illustrations copyright © 2013 Sandy Gingras
All rights reserved.

Sellers Publishing, Inc.
161 John Roberts Road, South Portland, Maine 04106
Visit our Web site: www.sellerspublishing.com
E-mail: rsp@rsvp.com

ISBN 13: 978-1-4162-0918-8

10 9 8 7 6 5 4 3 2 1

Printed and bound in China.

Living with Hope

by Sandy Gingras

SELLERS
PUBLISHING

Hope is sometimes easy to find. On sunny days, it's shining all around us. It's in the opening of a flower, in a butterfly's emergence from a cocoon, in the way the butterfly lands in our hands ever so

gently.

"We are cups, constantly and quietly being filled."

-Ray Bradbury

But, sometimes life gets dark, and hope is harder to find, harder to see. (It's like, just when you need it most, your flashlight goes out...).

Let this little book be a kind of flashlight. And let's go find hope together.

Because we know it's right
here-- Within ourselves and
our lives. We are all "living
with hope" every day...

A friend of mine has cancer. She says, it's "popping up like daisies" in her body. When she tells me this, I imagine a whole field of fear. How can we get through such darkness as this?

Where is the ROAD?

"We walk through night,
'til night is a poem."
— Brenda Hillman

I hold her hand,
because we are not meant
to be alone.

And so we walk, as all journeys small and large go... Our humanity is made

in moments.

practice tenderness.

Forgive each other.

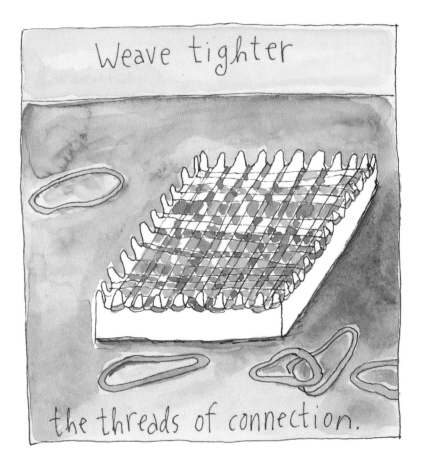

Weave tighter the threads of connection.

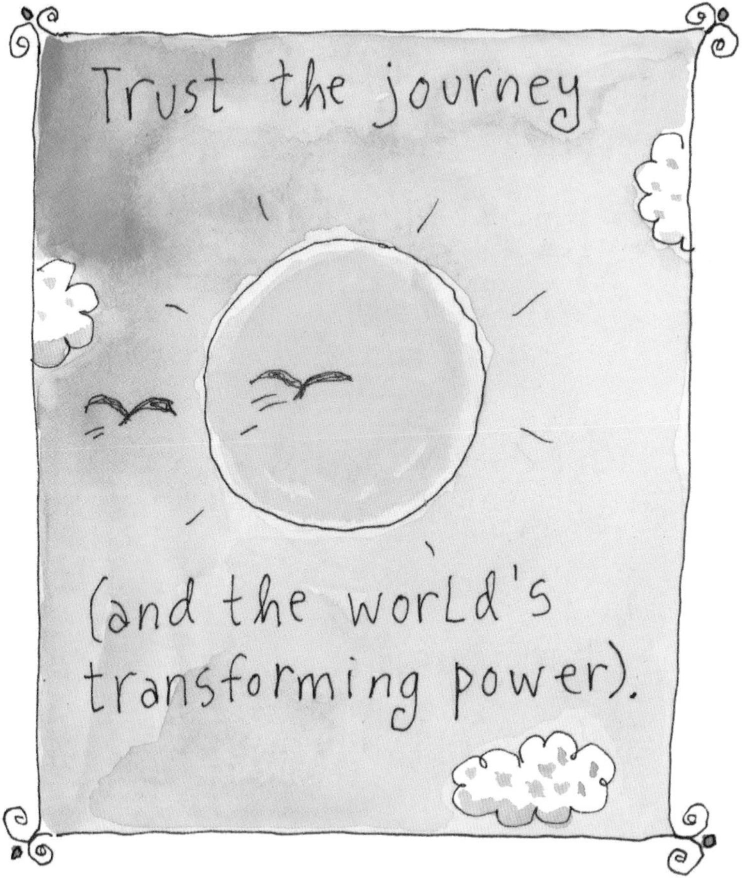
Trust the journey
(and the world's transforming power).

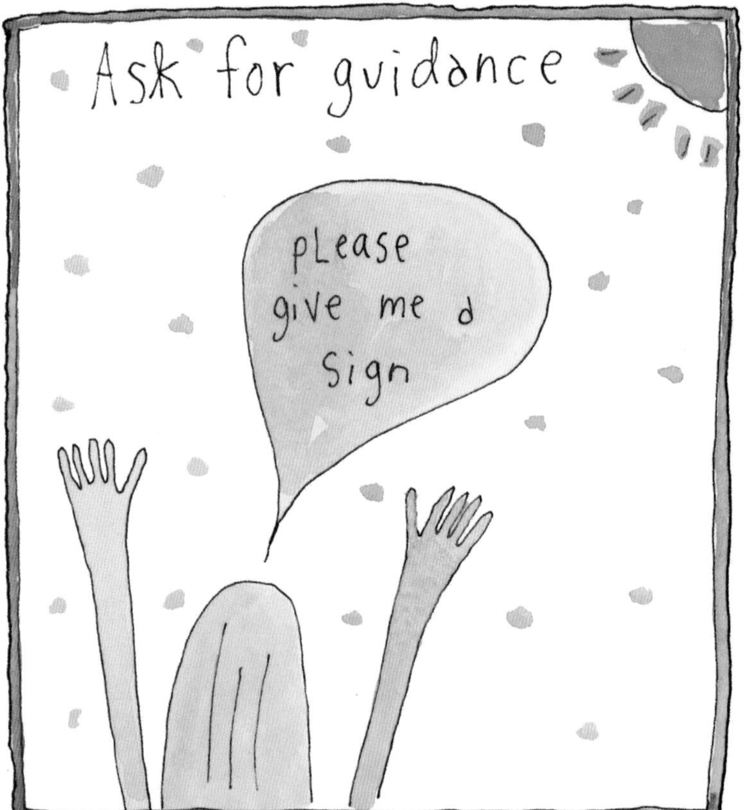
Ask for guidance
please give me a sign

and know that

is the message
you'LL receive.

Gestures of love are like indelible ink. We write on each other's hearts every day.

Our messages matter.
They add up to our life
story.

Often, when we are in pain, our instinct is to protect ourselves, to shut our doors to the world. We feel CLOSED victimized, overwhelmed and like we can't endure more. But, this is the time to open ourselves to emotion, to

This is not magic.

yet it **IS** magic.

Remember
that
fear
is
the
opposite
of
Life.

Sticky note to self:

TO DO:
life
without
hesitation

But which way do we go in the darkness? We literally **FEEL** our way... We follow our hearts, Listen to what Love tells us to do.

We "live out the confusions 'til they become clear."
-Anaïs Nin

When we are facing darkness, we often feel helpless and like our gestures are too small or inadequate...

Or we just don't know what to say or do.

As Mother Teresa says, "Be faithful in small things, because it is in them that your strength lies."

That is the
loveliness
That is the
sweetness
Use what powers and
talents you have (and
don't self-judge).

"The woods would be very silent if no birds sang except those who sang best."

-Henry Van Dyke

And that is, in itself,
a present.

"I've learned that people will forget what you said, people will forget what you did, but people will never forget how you made them feel."

—Maya Angelou

Practice gratitude for now, even when now is difficult. People have the most tender and alive moments in the worst of times. Be open to the possibility of blessedness arriving unexpectedly.

"the doorbell rings...
It's the present moment."

"Whatever the present moment contains, accept it as if you had chosen it... This will miraculously transform your whole Life."
—Eckhart Tolle

We often think that the future is where hope resides, but it really exists in the present. When you live your life in the present moment, fully and lovingly, Life suddenly becomes more peaceful and simple.

In bad times, I always say this to myself: "I am eternally grateful for the abundance that is mine." It reminds me of what is full in my life when I am feeling loss, and reminds me to feel thankful when I am feeling hopeless.

Ask for help.
and so I really don't know what to do...
There are earth angels..
Ask one to tea...

Send hope an invitation.

Please come to my
house and bring
your unending light.

Leave your door open.

Breathe.
Be your own rainbow of energy.

aah...

Try imagining a calm "positive" color entering your body with every inhale, a "negative" color leaving with every exhale, and allow the colors to change.

And if now gets to be too difficult to bear, remember that Life is made to change. The tide comes in again. The night runs out of darkness, the clouds run out of rain. The stars that looked blue shine brightly again.

Trust that Love is Invincible.

That Life is full of Miracles.

"Never
never

never

give
up."

—Winston Churchill

And when you feel that you are not strong enough, remember that vulnerability is strength, gentleness is strength. To feel broken is often to be most wholly and powerfully human...

"If God showed us the distance from where we are to where we're going, we'd think it was too far."

−IyanLa VanZant

Shine your Light

Share your Light.

Light a light for hope
and one for sorrow.
Light one for love
and one for loss.
Light one for me
and one for you.

We'll light our hearts together in the field of darkness, and make bright the walk of this world.